The Fi[illegible] STORYBOOK COLLECTION

MACDONALD YOUNG BOOKS

This edition first published in Great Britain in 1995 by
Macdonald Young Books Ltd
Campus 400
Maylands Avenue
Hemel Hempstead HP2 7EZ

Printed and bound in Portugal by Ediçocs ASA

ISBN 0 7500 1784 8

Contents

Emily's Legs 5

William's Problems 49

The Great Aunt Izzy Disaster 93

Magic Mark 137

Dick King-Smith

Emily's Legs

Illustrated by Katinka Kew

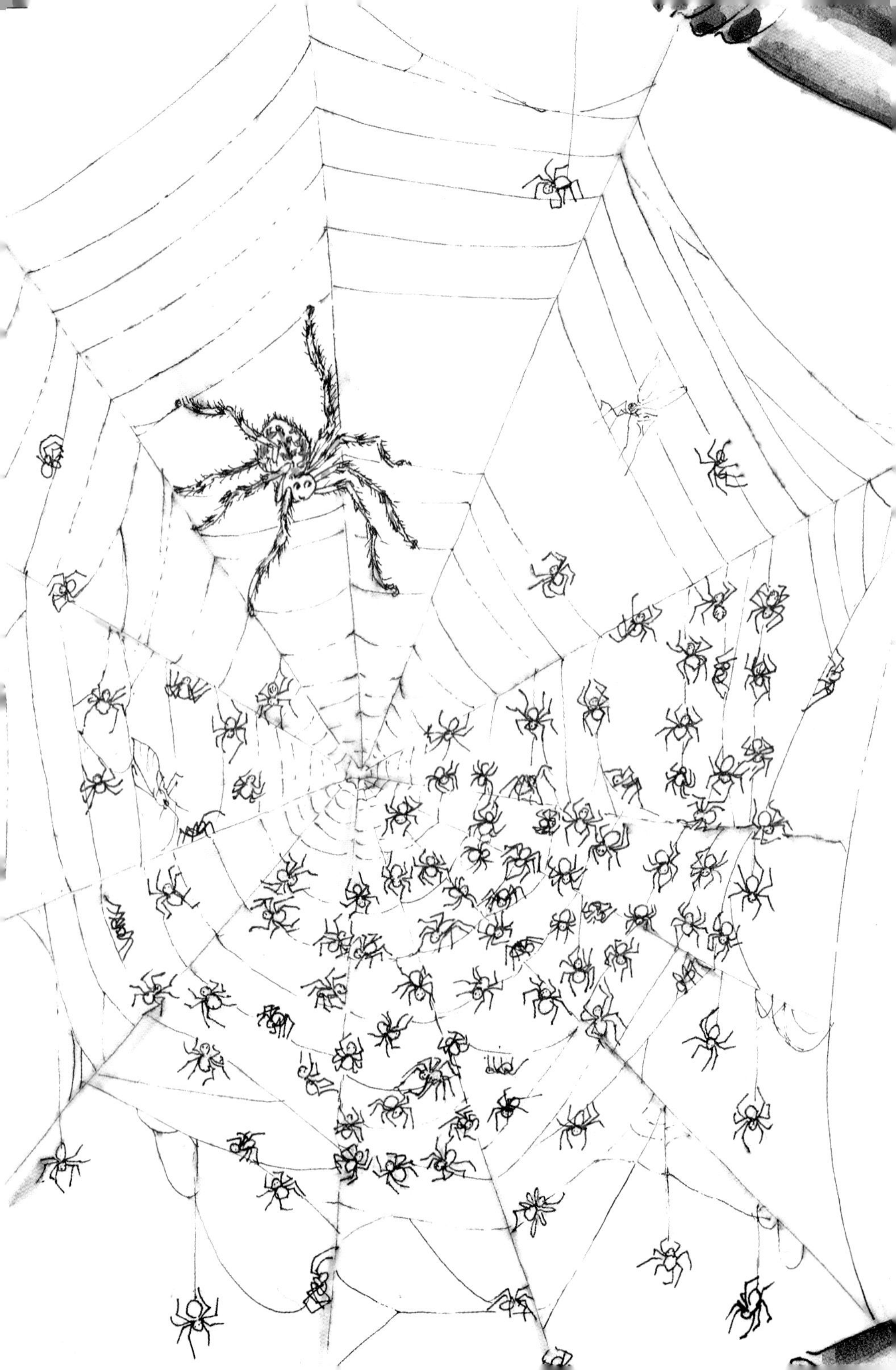

Chapter One

To begin with, nobody noticed.

Mind you, you couldn't blame Mother Spider. If she'd only had one baby, she'd have been sure to notice.

But she had a hundred babies, all hatching out at the same time. How could she be expected to know that ninety-nine spiderlings were normal and one was different?

Father Spider didn't notice. For one thing, he didn't like children.

For another, he was always too busy sitting quite still, waiting for house-flies and bluebottles to land in his web, in the highest darkest corner of the room.

Emily's ninety-nine brothers and sisters didn't notice.

Nobody noticed, not even Emily, until the night of the Spider Sports.

For the grown-up spiders, there were lots of different events. There was web-spinning

(how quickly could you make a whole one from start to finish) and fly-parcelling (how quickly could you tie up a fly in silken threads) and fly-eating (how quickly could you... yes, well, I needn't explain that

And there was abseiling, where you let out a thread and whizzed down it from the ceiling, and thread-climbing, where you whizzed back up again.

But for the spiderlings there were only the eight-legged races.

Now this was where Emily's troubles began.

Not that she didn't run in the eight-legged races at the Spider Sports.

She did.

Not that she didn't win.

She did.

The trouble was that she won them all and she won them all so easily.

First, all the spiderlings were lined up at one end of the room, and they had to race across the carpet to the other end.

Emily won easily.

Then they had to race up the wall of the room.

Emily won easily.

Then they had to race down the wall.

Emily won easily.

Last of all was the upside-down eight-legged race, right across the ceiling.

Yes, you've guessed, Emily won easily.

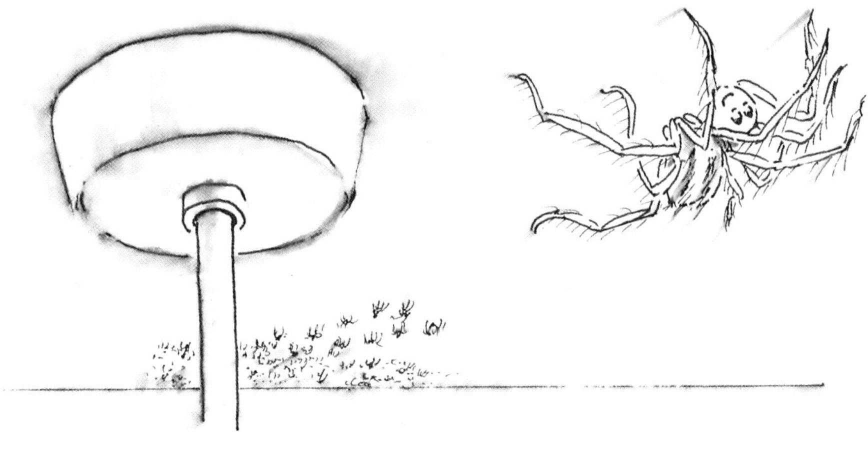

"Amazing!" said all the grown-up spiders. "Well done, Emily!"

But the spiderlings weren't so happy.

"Why does Emily *always* win?" they asked one another.

"Why does Emily *always* win?" they asked the grown-up spiders.

"Because she's the fastest, of course," said the grown-up spiders in the knowing way that old folk have.

"But *why* is she the fastest?" asked the spiderlings in the annoying way that young folk have. And that was when the truth was discovered.

Emily was asked to appear in front of the Spider Sports Committee to receive her prizes, four neatly parcelled little flies.

"Congratulations, Emily," said the chairperson of the Sports Committee. "You have won all four eight-legged races. Why is that, do you think?"

"If you please," said Emily (for she was by nature a polite spiderling), "it's because I ran the fastest."

"Ah!" said a very old grown-up spider. "But *why* did you run the fastest?"

Emily scratched her head with her two front legs. "I don't really know," she said modestly. "I suppose I just legged it quicker than they did."

"Legged it?" said the very old grown-up spider.

"Legged it?" said all the other grown-up spiders.

And they all looked carefully at Emily's legs.

They weren't any different from the legs of all the other spiderlings. They were no longer. They were no stronger. They were no hairier. But suddenly they all saw that, though Emily was scratching her head with her two front legs, yet she was still standing on eight others.

Emily had ten legs!

Chapter Two

For a moment nobody spoke.

Then, "Disgraceful!" said the very old grown-up spider.

"Disgusting!" cried the chairperson of the Sports Committee.

"Disqualified!" shouted all the other grown-up spiders.

Then Emily was made to hand back the four neatly parcelled fly-prizes, and the Committee scuttled off to spread the news.

When Mother Spider heard it, she went straight up the wall.

"Egbert!" she shouted. "Egbert!" (for that was Father Spider's name). "Where are you?"

Father Spider was where he always was, in the highest darkest corner of the room.

At first he did not answer. His wife sounded angry. Like most of his kind, he was a good deal smaller than she was. A number of his old friends had disappeared, suddenly and completely, on account of their wives being angry.

Or hungry.

Or both.

He tensed himself for a quick getaway, and as he saw his large wife approaching, he called out in a syrupy voice, "Why, Muriel," (for that was Mother Spider's name). "Whatever is the matter, dearest?"

"Oh Egbert!" cried Mother Spider. "It's Emily!"

"Who is Emily?"

"One of our children. Oh, the little wretch! Oh the shame! Oh, I'm so embarrassed!"

"Why?"

"She has ten legs," said Mother Spider in a horrified voice.

Now as soon as Father Spider was sure that his wife was not angry with *him*, he changed his tune completely.

"Look here, Muriel," he said sternly. "First of all, you know that I don't like children. Second, I couldn't care less how many legs they have - she's lucky, this Emily, she's got a couple of spares. And third, I object to being interrupted when I'm busy."

"But you're not doing anything."

"Yes, I am. I'm busy sitting still, waiting for house-flies and bluebottles. Kindly go away!"

Meanwhile Emily sat silent, alone with her thoughts. She had counted her legs carefully, first clockwise, then anti-clockwise, but the answer came out the same either way – ten.

Emily felt sad, as anyone would who had been disqualified and had her prizes taken away and been shouted at by a Sports Committee.

And Mother and Father will be angry too, I suppose, she thought. Grown-ups! They're all the same.

Then she cheered up a bit. At least my brothers and sisters won't care, she thought. I'll go down to the Gym and have some fun. And off she scuttled (very fast, of course).

The Gym was an old dusty cupboard, where the spiderlings gathered to practise making their first very small webs, and to do abseiling and climbing and generally enjoy themselves. A number of large disused webs hung across the cupboard, and these acted as safety-nets for those who fell by mistake, and trampolines for those who fell on purpose.

Ten or a dozen spiderlings were in the Gym when Emily arrived, but the moment they saw her, they all stopped doing whatever they were doing and stared at her in silence.

Then one of them spoke.

"Cheat!" it said in a nasty voice. "You're a cheat!"

And then the rest joined in.

"Who's a clever girl then?"

"Won all the races!"

"The eight-legged races!"

"But she's got ten legs!"

"Cheat! Cheat! Dirty cheat!"

"I didn't know," Emily said. "Honest, I didn't know I had ten," but they went on yelling, which made her angry.

"Anyway," she said, "I bet I could beat you lot with two legs tied behind my back."

At this, there was once again silence in the Gym. Then the first spiderling spoke again in a voice that was even nastier.

"You're never going to be given the chance," it said. "Come on, everybody. Get her!"

Chapter Three

Emily ran out of the Gym as fast as her ten legs would carry her. She ran down the wall, dashed across the carpet, and hid in a crack in the skirting-board. She waited, facing outwards. The crack was narrow, so that they would only be able to come at her one at a time.

"I'll jolly well show 'em," she said to herself. "Calling me a cheat. They'd better be careful."

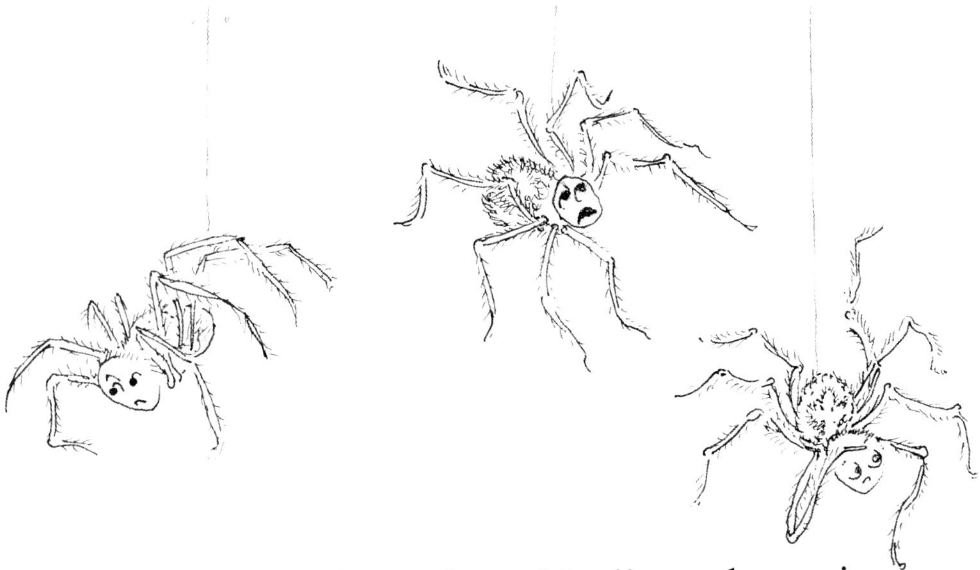

She could hear the spiderlings chattering to each other as they ran about the room in search of her.

"Wait till we find her!"

"We'll make her wish she'd never been hatched!"

"We'll show her!"

"We'll show Miss Emily Ten-legs!"

"Let's pull off one of them!"

"Let's pull off two! Then she'd be a proper spider!"

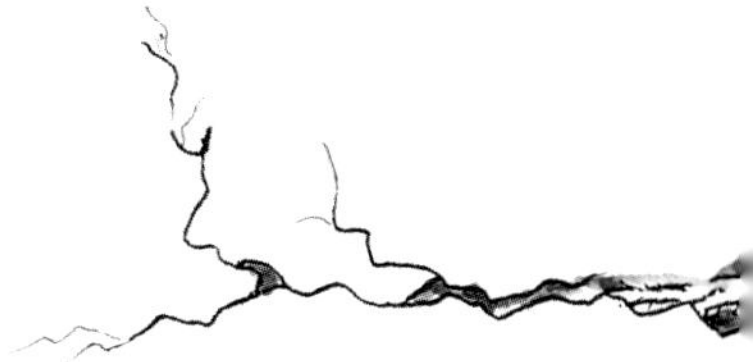

You just try it, thought Emily. I'm not afraid of you.

But she was, and it was a great relief to hear her mother's voice, calling angrily to the others.

"What are you doing, you naughty children?" she cried to the gang of spiderlings.

"Just playing," they said.

"How many times have I told you not to play out in the room in broad daylight? Stay in the Gym, or under the chairs, or behind the curtains," said Mother Spider.

Then she used the threat that mother spiders everywhere use to frighten their naughty children.

"If you're not careful," she said, "the Hoover will get you! Now scuttle off, the lot of you!"

Emily waited till the spiderlings had gone, and then she came out of her hole. I'd better face the music, she thought. She can't eat me, after all. Or can she?

"Mother?" she said, a little nervously.

Mother Spider was hanging from the lampshade. She let out thread rapidly and came whizzing down to the floor. She did not look best pleased. Emily crossed two of her legs for luck.

Mother Spider walked all round her slowly. As she went, she counted out loud.

"So it's true," she said at last in a low voice. "It's true what they're saying. Never have I been so embarrassed."

"I didn't know, Mother," said Emily. "Honest, I didn't know I had ten."

"Nor did I," said Mother Spider. "But now that I do, I've only one thing to say to you."

"What's that?"

"Never darken my web again!" said Mother Spider, and she reeled in thread and shot up into the lampshade without a backward look.

Emily sighed. Perhaps my father will be kinder, she thought. She had never met him, but she knew where he lived.

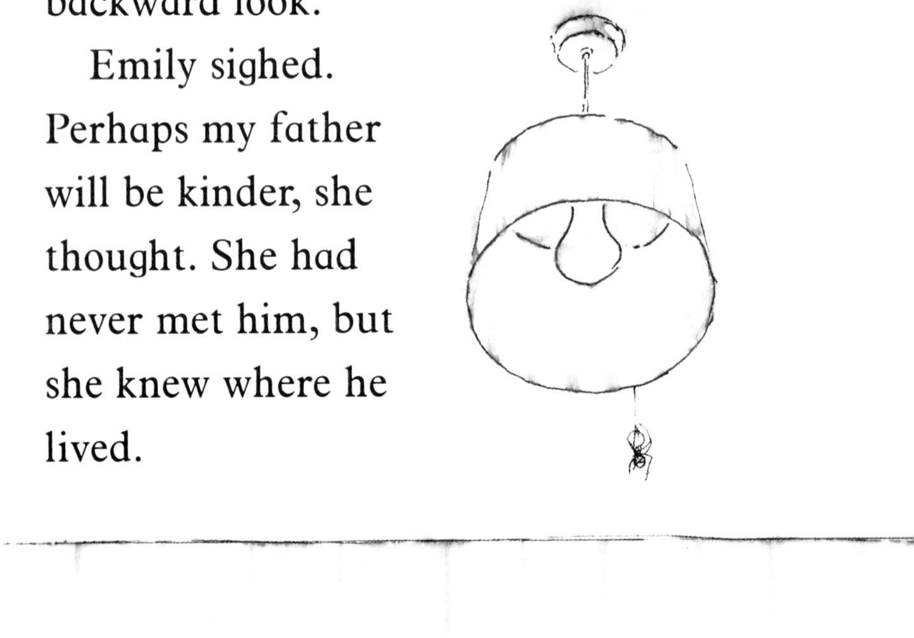

She ran round the edge of the room, keeping a sharp eye out for other spiderlings, and began to climb to the highest darkest corner.

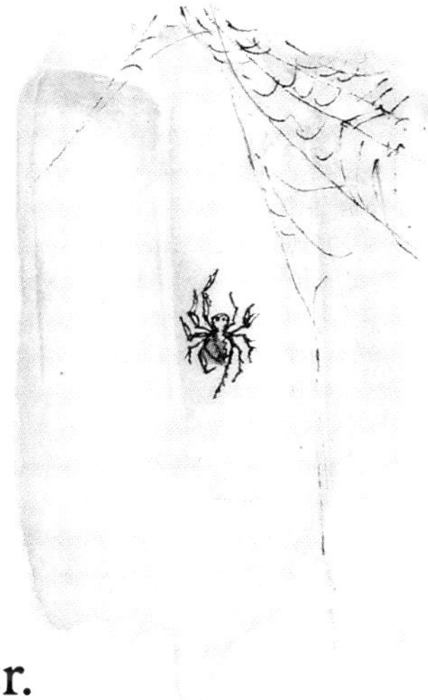

Father Spider was busy sitting still when he felt a slight shudder on his web. He dashed out, to find, not a house-fly or a bluebottle, but a spiderling.

"Father?" said Emily, a little nervously.

"Go away!" said Father Spider crossly.

"You know I don't like children."

"But I'm your daughter."

"I have hundreds of daughters," said Father Spider, "and hundreds of sons, and I don't like any of them."

"But I'm Emily."

"The one with ten legs?"

"Yes," said Emily.

"I didn't know, Father," she said. "Honest, I didn't know I had ten."

"What are you moaning about?" said Father Spider. "Think yourself lucky. You've got a couple of spares."

He pulled back the thread on which Emily was standing.

"Get lost!" he said, and he let it go with a twang.

Emily was hurled from the web like a stone from a catapult.

At the same time the room was filled with a sudden roaring noise, a noise that grew louder as Emily fell until, as she hit the floor, it was very loud indeed.

And very close.

Dazed and helpless, Emily could only watch as the monster rushed towards her.

Her mother's words echoed in her brain.

"The Hoover will get you!"

Chapter Four

In time to come, when Emily was herself a mother spider, her own spiderlings often asked her for a web-time story. And their favourite was 'The Day The Hoover Ate Mum.' They knew, because they had heard it so often, that it had a happy ending.

But a happy ending was the last thing Emily expected when she was sucked into the mouth of the vacuum cleaner.

The first thing she felt was a sharp pain (two sharp pains, to be exact).

Then she found herself in a thick choking blackness, unable to see or to cry out – for her eyes and mouth were full of dust – and unable to hear anything but the dreadful deafening noise of the machine. For a moment, Emily thought she was dead.

But then the Hoover was switched off, the heap of fluff and dirt settled to the bottom of the bag, and Emily fought her way to the top of it.

To her surprise and relief she found she was not alone, for suddenly a voice rang out in the darkness.

"All clear, my lads!" it cried. "Us can unroll now."

Once her eyes had grown accustomed to the darkness, Emily could see that the speaker was a large wood-louse, and that several other wood-lice had climbed to the top of the pile of dust. They looked at Emily in a friendly manner.

"Hullo, young 'un," said the first wood-louse. "You'm looking a bit gloomy."

"I am," said Emily. "Nobody likes me. Not my mother nor my father nor my horrid brothers and sisters."

"Whyever not?"

"Because I've got ten legs."

"Poor little mite!" cried the wood-louse. "Only ten!"

"Why d'you say 'only' ten?" said Emily.

"Because you should have fourteen by rights. All wood-lice has fourteen legs."

"But she's not a wood-louse," said a voice behind Emily. "She's a spider."

Emily turned round to see a spiderling, a little smaller than herself, emerging from the dust-pile.

"Who are you?" she said.

"My name's James," said the spiderling. "What's yours?"

"Emily," said Emily. "I hope you're not one of my brothers?"

"I hope not," said James. "They don't sound very nice."

"They're not," said Emily. "They're horrible to me. And so are my sisters. And so are my mother and father."

"What are your parents' names?" said James.

"Muriel and Egbert."

"Never heard of them."

"Good. Then you can't be related to me."

"No," said James.

"But when we get out of here, I'd like to be," and he put one of his legs round Emily's waist.

"Oh don't be so soppy!" cried Emily, pushing him away. "Anyway, we're never going to get out of here."

"Oh yes you will, young 'un!" cried the wood-lice.

"All you got to do is wait..."

"... till they empties the Hoover bag..."

"... into the dustbin..."

"... and then you climbs up the inside of it..."

"... and the next time they do take the lid off..."

"... out you pops!"

"But when will they empty it?" said Emily.

"Soon, I should think," said James. "It's pretty full," and hardly were the words out of his mouth when they all felt the Hoover being lifted, and carried away, and set down again.

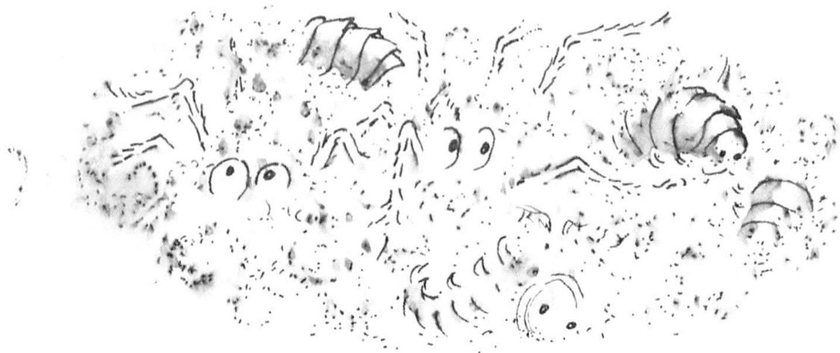

Then they heard the zip of the outer cover being undone, and the thick paper bag in which they were all imprisoned shook.

"Watch out, my lads!" shouted the first wood-louse. "We'm a-going!"

"Quickly, Emily," said James. "Attach safety-lines!"

He was only just in time, because at that moment the bottom of the paper bag was opened, and dirt and dust and fluff and wood-lice fell into the dustbin.

The bag was empty, save for the two spiderlings suspended within it; and before it could be closed again Emily and James let out thread, swung themselves to the side of the dustbin, and scampered up the wall of it and over the rim and away.

They scuttled for the nearest cover and crouched there breathlessly till all was quiet again.

Then James began to stare at Emily's legs.

Next, he walked all round her slowly. As he went, he counted out loud.

"Oh don't *you* start!" cried Emily. "If you don't like me having ten legs, you can jolly well push off!"

James stopped at the count of eight.

"You haven't," he said.

"Haven't what?"

"Haven't got ten legs. You've got eight. Same as any other spider."

And then Emily remembered the sharp pain (two sharp pains, to be exact) as the Hoover had sucked her in.

"Except you're not the same as any other spider, Emily," said James. "You're prettier. I think it would be nice if we set up web together," and once again he put one of his legs round Emily's waist.

"Oh don't be so soppy!" cried Emily. But this time she did not push him away.

"And anyway," said James, "they'll grow again."

"What will?"

"The two legs you lost. Spiders of our sort can do that."

"How d'you know?"

"My dad's done it. Mum lost her temper with him one day and pulled off one of his, and he grew a lovely new one."

"Gosh!" said Emily excitedly. "Then I'll still be the fastest spider of them all!"

"Yes."

"But oh!" said Emily miserably. "You won't like me any more, James. Not with ten legs."

"Emily," said James. "When legs are as beautiful as yours, you cannot possibly have too many of them," and he stroked one of hers with one of his.

"Oh James!" said Emily happily. "You say the soppiest things!"

William's Problems

Shirley Isherwood

Illustrated by Jill Bennett

PENCILS

Chapter One

William Barnes had problems.

Problem number one was that he couldn't always get his b's and d's the right way round.

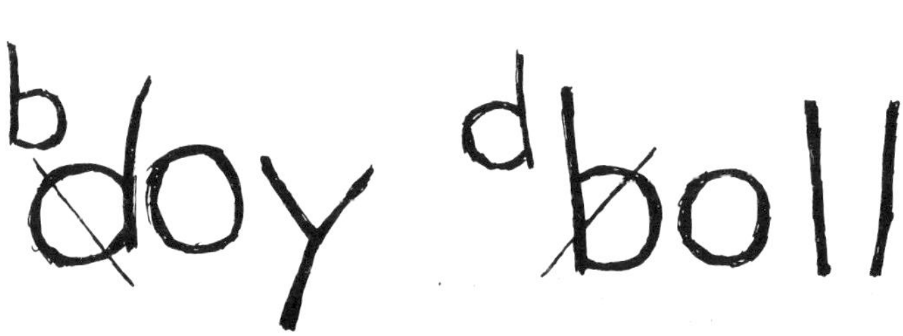

Problem number two was that his father had gone to work away from home, and William missed him. But that wasn't such a bad problem, because he'd soon be coming back.

William and his mother talked about him a lot, and about how wonderful it would be when he came home. It made them feel much happier.

They told William's little brother Matthew about how wonderful it would be. But Matthew was only one year old, and didn't seem to care one way or another. He just smiled and waved his rattle. When you are only one you don't have many problems, thought William. William was seven.

But problem number three was the biggest problem of all. William's grandfather was coming to live with them, and William would have to give up his nice big bedroom, so that Grandfather could move into it.

It was a wonderful room, and William loved it. It was big enough

for him to be able to set out his model railway, and still have enough space to leave all his other toys lying about. William's habit of leaving his toys lying about was a problem, said his mother.

But William didn't think it was a problem – it was just handy.

The day came when Grandfather and his furniture would arrive. William and his mother sat in the kitchen.

It was the last time that they would have breakfast alone.

As he ate his breakfast, William thought about his grandfather. He hadn't met him very many times

because Grandfather lived a long way off, right at the other end of the country.

But now he was coming to live in William's bedroom.

"Why?" asked William.

"He's lonely," said William's mother.

"Is being lonely a problem?" said William.

"It can be," said his mother.

William went to school. In the middle of the morning his teacher asked everyone to write a story about an animal.

William thought that he would write a story about a bad dog, who went round digging in gardens, and barking at everyone.

Then he remembered the b's and d's. If he got them the wrong way round it might not say 'bad dog,' but 'dab bog' – which was silly.

So he wrote a story about a ginger cat instead.

It was quite boring.

Then he went home and found a van standing outside the house. Grandfather's furniture had arrived.

Chapter Two

William went to look at his old room. It was full of chests and a huge, old bed. The furniture almost filled the room.

"There will hardly be room for him to move about!" said William's mother.

"Why doesn't he get smaller furniture?" asked William.

"He's had these things a long time," said William's mother. "He's very fond of them. He doesn't want to give them up. It's a problem."

William went to look at his new room. It was very small and tidy – for there was no room to leave his things lying about.

William liked to see his things lying about, and he understood how Grandfather felt about his old chests and his bed. But all the same he grumbled about his new little room all the way through tea.

After tea, Grandfather arrived. He came from the station by taxi, and he made the taxi driver sound the horn, to let everyone know that he was there.

Then he came stamping up the hall, and into the kitchen, and said "Hallo!" to everyone in a loud voice.

Every time he spoke his voice was loud. And he seemed to stare a lot, with his very blue eyes. He stared at William, and William's mother, and at Matthew and the cat.

“Does he always shout and stare at people?” asked William, when his mother tucked him into bed that night.

“Always,” said his mother. “He’s always been like that.”

“Is it a problem?” asked William; for he wasn’t sure if he liked his grandfather’s way of shouting and staring.

"Not when you get used to it," said his mother.

William lay in bed, and wondered if he'd ever get used to problems.

He wondered if he'd ever get used to putting his things away neatly.

He wondered if he'd ever get used to the problem of the b's and d's.

He wondered if he'd ever get used to the new noises which came from Grandfather's bedroom – the twanging sound of the springs of the bed and the sudden loud snores.

But the next evening, William found that they really did have a problem. Grandfather began to play his tuba in his bedroom. It made a big, deep noise, which filled the whole house. Then it began to play a low, rumpty-tumpty sort of tune.

William rather liked the music. It was the sort of noise, he thought, that a happy lion might make, if a lion could sing.

But the neighbours didn't like it. Mrs Dart knocked on the wall. Mr Humber came to William's house and said that he couldn't hear his television for the noise. The noise also woke Matthew up, and he began to cry.

"I don't know what we are going to do," said William's mother. "Grandfather loves playing his tuba. It will be really sad if he has to stop."

But Grandfather didn't stop playing the tuba. He just said "Rubbish!" when William's mother told him about the people next door.

"Everyone likes to hear a bit of music," he said. And he played every night – first the lion tune, and then a march, and then a very slow waltz, which made William think of big, black seals, walloping over in the water.

The neighbours kept complaining, and Matthew kept on waking up.

Then one night, between the lion tune and the march, William put a tape on his cassette player. The tape had been playing for a moment, when his grandfather knocked on the wall. William was very angry.

He went to his grandfather's room, where his grandfather sat on the edge of his bed, holding the tuba.

"*You* make a noise," said William. "Why can't I make a noise?"

"Children should be seen and not heard," said his grandfather.

William marched down the stairs and told his mother. "He said that children should be seen and not heard,"

he said. "What does that mean?"

"That's how children were meant to be when he was a little boy," said William's mother. "They were meant to sit quietly and not make a sound."

"Did he sit quietly?" asked William

"I don't suppose so," said his mother.

"Then why does he want me to do it?" said William.

"Oh, William!" said his mother. "Don't pester. I've got enough problems!"

Chapter Three

The next day was just as bad. At school, William got all his b's and d's the wrong way round.

His teacher tried to help him. "Draw the stick and then the circle to make a b," he said. "And draw the circle and then the stick to make a d."

But still William couldn't remember which way was which when he came to write the letters down.

"William Barnes is *stupid,*" said a boy in William's class.

"No, I'm *not,*" said William, and he went home in a bad temper, feeling very unhappy.

At home he found that Matthew was in a bad temper too, because

he was tired after being woken up in the night by Grandfather's tuba. He was crying, and William's mother was trying to soothe him.

She wasn't in a very good temper either, and she didn't seem to listen when William tried to tell her about the b's and d's going wrong, and about being called stupid. And it was all because of his grandfather, thought William.

William went out into the garden, and decided that everything was awful, and that he would run away from home. He ran off down the street, round the corner, and into the park.

But, once in the park, there didn't seem to be anywhere else to go. He went into the playground, but there was no one on the swings. Everyone was at home, having tea. William wandered round and round, feeling lonely, a bit frightened, and very hungry.

Then he began to run again – and as he went down the broad path, he saw his grandfather.

He was sitting on a bench, and when he saw William, he stuck out his walking stick, so suddenly that William almost fell over it.

"What are *you* doing here?" said William's grandfather.

"I'm running away!" said William.

"Why?" said his grandfather.

"I've got problems," said William.

"So have I," said his grandfather.

William was surprised. He had never thought of his grandfather having problems. He sat down on the bench and looked at him.

"What's your problem?" said William's grandfather.

William didn't like to say, "It's you!" So he said, "I can't get b's and d's the right way round."

"That's an easy problem to solve," said William's grandfather, and he took a notebook and a pencil from his pocket. "All you have to do," he said, "is draw a little bed, like this."

He drew a bed, with the stick of the b making the head of the bed, and the stick of the d making the foot. The circles of the letters made the middle of the bed.

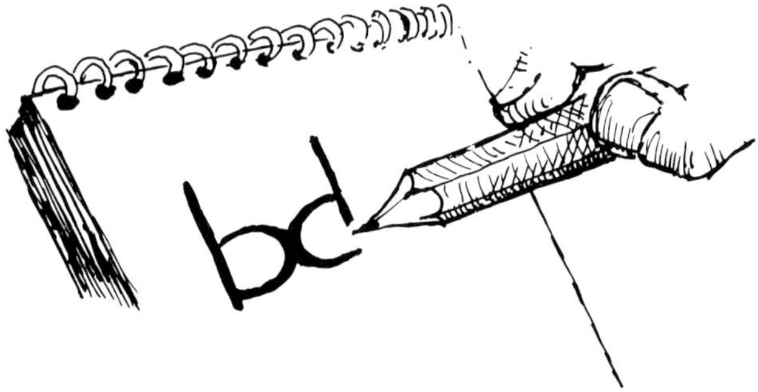

Then he drew a little stick-man on the bed, with his head on the b and his feet on the d. Like this:

William took the notebook and the pencil and turned to a clean page.

Then he thought of the little bed, and made the b and d. They were the right way round, said his grandfather.

So William thought of other words with the letters b and d, and thought of the little bed and got the letters right. It was wonderful. One of his problems was solved.

Grandfather put away the notebook and they both got up and began to walk down the path.

William turned to look at his grandfather. "What's your problem?" he said.

"Living in someone else's house," said his grandfather. "That's my problem."

Chapter Four

William was more surprised than ever. William's problem was that his grandfather was living with him. And now his grandfather said that *his* problem was living with William.

They both had the same problem really, thought William.

"Don't you *like* living with us?" he asked.

"It's fine!" said his grandfather. "It just takes a little getting used to."

They turned round, and began to make their way back home for tea.

"Were you seen and not heard when you were a little boy?" said William, as they went.

"No," said his grandfather, "and I don't suppose that you will be – will you?"

"No," said William.

"Then I'll stop asking you," said his grandfather.

They went a little further, and then his grandfather spoke again.

"Sorry you got booted out of your room, William," he said.

"That's all right," said William. "I'll get used to it."

But there was still the problem of the tuba-playing. Everyone had a talk about it after tea – and it was William who solved the problem.

"Why don't you play in the morning?" he said. "Everyone's awake then, so the noise wouldn't matter."

"What a good idea!" said William's grandfather.

So they asked Mrs Dart and Mr Humber if they would mind if Grandfather played his tuba in the morning, and they both said, "Not at all!"

The next morning, before he went to school, William heard his grandfather play the lion song, and the walloping seal waltz. He whistled the tunes all the way to school.

In the afternoon his teacher asked everyone to write about someone they knew. William decided he would write about his grandfather.

'My grandfather has come to live with us,' he wrote. 'I didn't think I liked him at first. It gives you a bad feeling when someone lives with you, and you don't like them. But now I like him a lot better. I think he likes me. He still shouts when he talks, but my mother says he's always done that, so he isn't going to stop. He stares at you a lot, but I think that's just because he likes to have a good look at things.'

William's teacher liked what William had written. "It's very good, William," he said. "And you've got all your b's and d's the right way round. Well done!"

"No problem!" said William.

Denny Robson

THE GREAT AUNT IZZY DISASTER

Illustrated by Jan Lewis

Chapter One

Emmeline Mary McGinty was a bucketful of trouble. At least her Great Aunt Izzy said so. The same Great Aunt Izzy was a stuffy old sock. At least Emmeline Mary said so.

Emmeline Mary McGinty liked cheeseburgers, pop songs, cartoons and knock knock jokes.

Great Aunt Izzy made cucumber sandwiches for tea, liked hymns in the evenings, and thought that children should be very quiet indeed.

So it wasn't really surprising that Emmy and Great Aunt Izzy didn't get on very well. And perhaps it wasn't so surprising that something rather strange happened the time Great Aunt Izzy came to stay.

"But why," moaned Emmy for the sixtieth time to Sam, her next door neighbour, "has *Aunt Izzy* been sent to look after me while Mum and Dad are away?"

Sam ignored her and continued waving a shiny pendant in front of Emmy's eyes. His dad had been hypnotised into giving up smoking and he was wondering whether he could hypnotise Emmy into giving up Aunt Izzy moans.

"She doesn't seem to like me much," Emmy went on, "and I think she's very odd."

It was true Aunt Izzy wasn't like anyone else. She was a tall thin old lady, with lines on her forehead you could play noughts and crosses on, and huge big feet that she forced into tiny shoes to make them look dainty. (Emmy thought this was what made her grumpy – she was always much nicer with her slippers on.)

"You are feeling sleepy," said Sam, looking hopeful. Emmy was really going to be a pain this week unless he could make this hypnotising trick work.

Emmy went silent. Sam sat up expectantly.

"No I'm not," said Emmy suddenly, grabbing the pendant. "We're going to have to do something."

"We?" Sam sounded a bit worried. Emmy had got him into lots of trouble before with her funny ideas.

"If we don't, I'll go nuts," Emmy threatened. "I'll start to look like a cucumber sandwich, I'll stop telling you jokes. . . ."

"All right, all right," laughed Sam. "But what can we do?"

They were silent for a few minutes. And then they both looked at the pendant in Emmy's hand.

"We can't," whispered Sam.

"Yes we can," said Emmy. "You can hypnotise her, and when she's in a trance, I'll persuade her that she likes all the things that I like, and then we'll change her back before Mum and Dad get back!"

And that was how the Great Aunt Izzy disaster started. Sam knew there was no point in arguing with Emmy. She never listened. He was to come back after lunch and they would start work on Great Aunt Izzy then.

Chapter Two

"Back again, young man?" exclaimed Great Aunt Izzy, when Sam returned after lunch. "So soon? When I was a girl. . . ."

Aunt Izzy was very fond of "when I was a girl" stories (which were always about how hard and nasty life used to be).

Emmy was still struggling through her cucumber sandwiches.

“Now eat up the crusts, Emmeline,” Aunt Izzy boomed, “or you’ll never get hair like mine.” Emmy looked at Aunt Izzy’s corkscrew frizz and quietly stuffed the crusts into a pot plant.

“Before I ate crusts my hair was completely—”

“Aunt Izzy,” Emmy interrupted. “Sam and I are doing an experiment. We want to see if we can make you relax using this pendant.” Aunt Izzy looked suspicious.

"Er, it might make your feet hurt less," Emmy went on. Aunt Izzy, whose feet at that moment were squeezed into a minute pair of pink pumps, looked tempted.

"Well," she said sitting back in her chair. "It can't hurt, I suppose. . . ."

Sam began straight away, before she had time to change her mind.

"*You are feeling sleepy, Aunt Izzy,*" he said in a sing-song voice. Emmy giggled.

"*Very sleepy. . . .*"
he droned, beginning
to feel a bit silly.
And he was starting
to feel very
uncomfortable
indeed, when suddenly,
to his astonishment,
Aunt Izzy's chin
dropped
and she fell asleep!

"We've done it,
Emm!" Sam whispered,
staring at Aunt Izzy
in amazement. "She's
in a trance!"

But Emmy didn't
reply.

Emmy was fast
asleep as well.

"Wake up, Emmy," Sam hissed, as he shook her shoulders. But Emmy didn't move. "The book," he said to himself. "That's it."

He frantically flicked through the pages and read:

"To wake the patient, merely tell them who they are, and that they will awake when you click your fingers."

"Right," he said, turning to Aunt Izzy by mistake in his panic. "You're Emmeline Mary McGinty and you will wake up when I click my fingers!"

He clicked his fingers, and then looked up – to see Great Aunt Izzy waking up!

"Hiya Sam," yawned Aunt Izzy. "I must have dropped off. Is the old dragon in a trance yet?"

Sam froze with horror.

"Emmy McGinty," he said quickly to Emmy. "Wake up now. *Please!*"

Emmy opened her eyes and looked at Sam's panic-stricken face.

"She thinks she's you, Emmy," he said. "I've accidently hypnotised Aunt Izzy into thinking she's you!"

Chapter Three

It couldn't be true, thought Emmy, staring at Aunt Izzy. But Aunt Izzy certainly wasn't sitting up as straight as she usually did. She was sprawling all over her chair – rather like Emmy usually did, in fact. And she was whistling along to a pop song on the radio!

How could it have happened? Emmy needed to talk to Sam – alone.

"Um, Emmeline Mary," said Emmy, in what she hoped sounded like Aunt Izzy's voice. "I think you should leave the table."

"Might as well," Aunt Izzy giggled. "Can't take it with me."

Amazing, thought Emmy, she even sounds like me.

"Er, go into the other room, Emmeline," Emmy went on, "and see what's on the telly."

"I already know," said Aunt Izzy nudging Sam. "A goldfish bowl and a vase of flowers."

Emmy's eyes opened wider. That was just the sort of thing that she would have said! Aunt Izzy winked at Sam and went into the living room.

"What are we going to do?" groaned Sam. "This is disastrous."

Emmy was looking thoughtful.

"Don't worry," she said finally, with that look in her eye Sam knew always meant trouble. "We can change her back. But not yet. Not until tea-time. Until then, I'm going to be Aunt Izzy and she can be me!"

Chapter Four

Sam shook his head. No way. It was a dreadful idea! He opened his mouth to protest, but Emmy had already disappeared. He found her in the living room, a look of gleeful fascination on her face, watching Aunt Izzy prise off her shoes and put on her own old trainers.

"Amazing," Emmy whispered. "She even ties them like I do."

"We have to stop this, Emmy," Sam hissed from behind her shoulder.

"Incredible," she giggled, as Aunt Izzy's old bones began jumping around to the radio. "She even dances like I do!"

"And if we don't stop this, Emmy McGinty. . . ." Emmy turned round. She knew better than to ignore that tone in Sam's voice.

Sam could be very determined when he wanted to be.

She smiled sweetly. "Just got to go upstairs, Sam."

There was no time to lose. Emmy dashed upstairs and into Aunt Izzy's room. A long black dress hung on the door. She quickly put it on, hitched it up using her school tie as a belt, stuck one foot into a tiny purple satin shoe, yanked it off, decided to stick to trainers, tried to frizz her hair, gave up, pulled an old black hat over her plaits, and then she looked in the mirror. Perfect.

Now for the great outdoors, she thought, sliding silently down the bannisters. She tip-toed past the living room (where Aunt Izzy could be heard loudly singing along to the radio) and out of the front door, before Sam could stop her. She was going to enjoy being an old lady.

Outside, the first thing Emmy did was hobble up to a policeman and ask him if he could see her across the road. The policeman, who immediately recognised Emmy, told her he could see her a mile away looking like that, and walked away laughing.

Then Emmy decided to try out her disguise at the bus stop. A little old lady began to talk to her.

"How long do you think the bus will be?" asked the old lady, looking at her watch.

"About 25 metres I should think," said Emmy, with an innocent look.

The old lady frowned and tapped her hearing aid. She tried again.

"Windy, isn't it?"

"No, it's Thursday," said Emmy with a giggle, and headed off towards the corner shop with a mixture of skips and hobbles.

Mr Grim, the shopkeeper, was a miserable man who didn't like kids in his store. He never let Emmy choose fruit for herself and always gave her the most bruised apples. Well, he wouldn't dare be rude to her now, Emmy thought gleefully.

Emmy began to examine the apples, turning each one over carefully, while out of the corner of her eye she watched Mr Grim twitch impatiently.

But after she'd rearranged two boxes of Granny Smiths, Mr Grim was beginning to peer suspiciously under her hat. Emmy decided it was time to leave.

She started to hobble away, and then, when she was sure he was watching, she leap-frogged over a pile of banana boxes! Mr Grim was so surprised he sat back on his best tomatoes.

Chapter Five

Emmy smiled to herself. That had been fun. But on the way back, she began to feel a bit uneasy. Maybe she shouldn't have left Sam with Aunt Izzy like that. . . .

And when she got home, she began to feel distinctly worried. There was no trace of Sam, or of Great Aunt Izzy. Where on earth could they be? She hung the long dress back on Aunt Izzy's door, and then she dashed up the road again.

It didn't take long to find them. In fact, it would have been impossible to miss Great Aunt Izzy. There she was, in the playground, surrounded by a huge crowd of kids, hanging like a bat from the climbing frame, and whooping loudly for Sam to join her.

Emmy giggled and looked over to where Sam was sitting on the bench. Sam was whistling. Emmy knew what that meant. Sam always whistled when he sulked.

She sat down next to him. "Sorry I ran off, Sam. It was just too good to miss. . . ."

Sam whistled harder. He'd had a horrid afternoon. First of all, Aunt Izzy had made him dance to a pile of Emmy's records. And then she'd almost dragged him out of the house to the playground. And if that wasn't bad enough, every time he tried to look as if he wasn't with her, she whooped his name loudly. He whistled even harder.

Emmy put her arm through his, and pulled a range of his favourite faces. A smile began to twitch at the corners of his mouth.

"OK," he laughed. "OK. But help me get the old bat home!"

Great Aunt Izzy, however, had other ideas. She was having far too much fun to go home. She had organised all the kids into a very silly game of

"Grandmother's Footsteps" (in which everyone was the grandmother, except her), and she wasn't going to leave until she had won. And when Sam tried to take her arm, she giggled and disappeared up the climbing frame again.

Then things got worse. When they finally persuaded Aunt Izzy to leave the park, she stopped at the corner shop and refused to budge. The customers all stared at the strange old lady chanting "*Eeny, meeny, miney, mo*" at the oranges.

Emmy giggled nervously.

Suddenly Aunt Izzy picked up the oranges and began to juggle with them. Mr Grim came angrily out of his shop. It was that kid dressed up again.

"I'll teach you to juggle with my oranges," he shouted angrily.

"I wish you would," frowned Aunt Izzy as she dropped one. "I don't seem to be very good at it."

Mr Grim's face turned orange and beetroot (which nicely matched the display behind him). He grabbed hold of Aunt Izzy's shoulders, swung her round to face him – and his face now went pale. It *was* an old lady after all.

Leaving him stuttering and stammering, Aunt Izzy hitched up her skirt and leap-frogged over the banana boxes.

Sam had had enough. He grabbed Emmy and Aunt Izzy's hands and marched them both home. He was going to change Aunt Izzy back no matter what Emmy said. But what if he couldn't? He had a moment's panic. One Emmy was enough for anyone!

Chapter Six

However, hypnotising Great Aunt Izzy back into her normal self proved to be no problem after all. There were a couple of worrying moments when Sam thought the old lady wasn't going to wake up at all, but on the third click of his fingers Aunt Izzy sat up very straight and announced it was time for tea.

Sam sighed with relief. But Emmy felt sad that the afternoon was over. True, they hadn't managed to change Aunt Izzy at all, but it had been fun pretending to be an old lady and watching Aunt Izzy acting like her.

She giggled as she remembered Aunt Izzy swinging from the climbing frame, shouting orders to the other kids.

But did she really behave like that herself? Emmy frowned. She had to admit, Aunt Izzy had been a bit of a pain. . . .

She would have to try harder with the old battleaxe, Emmy decided uncomfortably. If she stopped telling so many jokes then perhaps she and Aunt Izzy would get on better.

Aunt Izzy silently put out the plates and cups.

"Does the knife go on my right hand or my left?" Emmy asked, knowing Aunt Izzy was keen on such things.

"Neither," said Aunt Izzy, with a twinkle in her eye. "It goes on the table, Emmeline."

Emmy looked astonished. That was just what she would have said! Maybe

Aunt Izzy hadn't been changed back properly. Emmy began to feel worried.

"Can I help you make the tea," asked Emmy. "Will the sandwiches be long?"

"No, sort of short and squarish," said Aunt Izzy, bringing in the sandwiches, and then laughing at Emmy and Sam's astonished faces.

"You know, I'm not as stuffy as I look," she said sitting down. "When I was a girl. . . ."

This time Emmy didn't interrupt, because the stories Aunt Izzy began to tell them were very different from those she had told before.

They were wonderful stories, all about the jokes Aunt Izzy and her friends used to play when they were young, and the exciting games they had had. Emmy and Sam listened in astonishment. Was this the same Great Aunt Izzy?

The more Emmy listened, the more she decided she liked Aunt Izzy. And the more Aunt Izzy talked, the more she seemed to enjoy herself.

"It's funny," said Aunt Izzy after a while. "I'd forgotten all those things until today. I wonder what made me remember?"

Emmy coughed and cleared the table.

Emmy was sad when the week was over. By the time her mum and dad got back, she and Aunt Izzy had become the best of friends. In fact, Emmeline Mary McGinty was now a dear funny girl who told wonderful jokes. At least her Great Aunt Izzy said so. And that same Great

Aunt Izzy was a brilliant storyteller and a pretty special Aunt. At least Emmeline Mary said so.

And so in the end the Great Aunt Izzy disaster wasn't such a disaster after all.

Helen Muir

MAGIC MARK

Illustrated by Sarah Lenton

For Simeon

MAGIC MARK

On George's birthday, his best present was a box of conjuror's tricks.

"When I grow up," he said, "I'm going to be a magician. Don't call me George any more. My name is Magic Mark."

George tried out the itching powder on Uncle Ray and dropped a stink bomb on the bus.

He could turn water into milk and make an egg disappear.

Best of all was the MAGIC WAND!

By the time bed-time came, George thought he could do anything.

"When I say the magic words," he told his mother, "You'll disappear."

"Goodness!" she replied.

He tapped her with the wand. "Abracadabra!" George shouted. But she was still there doing the washing up.

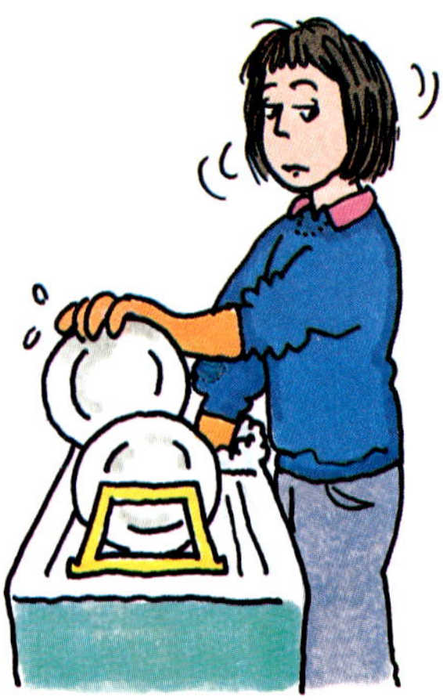

"Eat up, George," his father said, at breakfast.

"I can make this whole table disappear," George replied. "That'll surprise you."

He waved his wand and knocked the top off his father's boiled egg.

The breakfast table stayed where it was but George's father had egg on his shirt, egg in his hair and egg on his nose.

He *was* surprised.

So was George.

"You kids should call me Magic Mark now because I'm a magician," George told all his friends at school. "I can turn water into milk and make an egg disappear.

"If you call me George any more, I might turn you into crisps and King Cones. Then I'll eat you."

The other children laughed at Magic Mark. "Pooh! You can't turn anybody into crisps or icecream. You're not a real magician."

"One day," George promised, "I'll put you in a box and saw you in half." He muttered some mystericus words and dropped a stink bomb.

"If you were a proper magician, you'd be on television . . . so there," said a small girl called Emily. "I'm never going to call you Magic Mark because you're just stupid." She pulled a face at him and tapped her head rudely.

George put some itching powder on Emily's chair.

"Well, turn this old paint water into Coca Cola," Emily suggested, when the teacher went out of the room.

The children held their breath.

George turned his back to get his trick ready. He covered the conjuring container with the teacher's scarf.

"Hocus Pocus! Fish bones choke us!" he shouted, waving his arms. Red paint sploshed everywhere. There was a fearful mess.

But no Coca Cola.

THE

ONLY THING

TO DISAPPEAR

JUST THEN

WAS . . .

MAGIC MARK!

"When I say the magic words, all my tricks go wrong," George said sadly to his mother.

"I think it takes time to be a conjuror," she replied. "Let's go and see Giant Og, the magician in the Christmas pantomime. Everybody thinks he's marvellous!"

George was counting the days to the panto and some of his school friends were going on the same evening.

"I'm taking my magic wand and my best trick," he said. "Magicians always ask people to come onto the stage. Giant Og might want me to help him."

His best trick was turning water into milk. When the time came, George couldn't see any milk in the fridge so he filled his conjuring container with tomato ketchup.

The children loved the panto. When the beautiful Princess Zelda got lost in the wood, she wandered into the dark caves of Giant Og, the evil magician.

There was a roll of drums and a puff of smoke and the Giant appeared, with his man-sized Cat. "HOOH HOOH HAH!" he roared as he tied up the princess.

He stamped about and swallowed flames. He bent an iron bar and tore up telephone books. Then he sawed the princess in half and put her together again.

When the Giant asked who was brave enough to come up and rescue the princess, George got there first. The Cat helped him onto the stage.

Giant Og crouched down to look at his conjuring trick and wand. "Another magician, eh? And what's *your* name?" he boomed.

"Magic Mark," George answered, a bit shakily. "I can turn water into tomato ketchup."

"All right, Magic Mark! So you're going to save the lovely Princess Zelda, are you?" The Giant threw back his head and laughed.

"OH NO HE WON'T!" he roared to the audience.

"OH YES HE WILL!" the children yelled back.

The Giant cracked his knuckles. "I shall tie Princess Zelda in a sack and throw her in my cellar!"

She gave a little cry. "Help!"

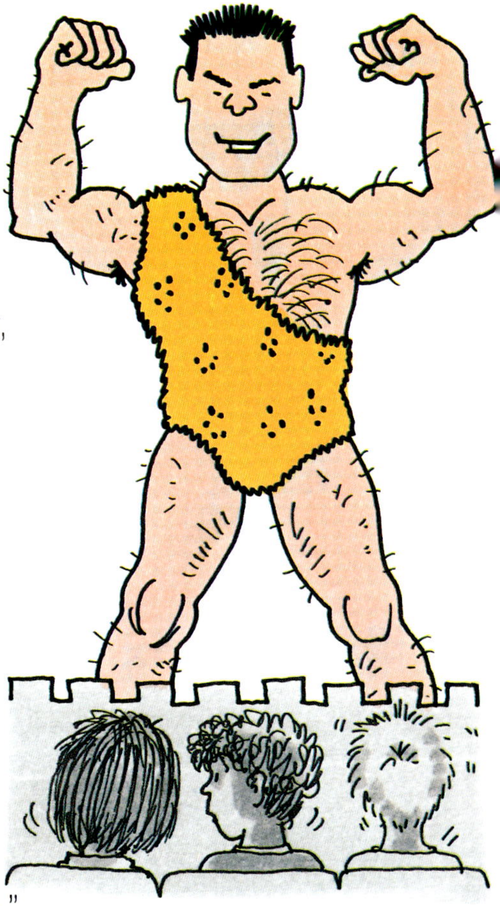

"Ha, ha! Nobody can escape me. *Nobody*. I can escape from handcuffs and iron chains because I am Giant Og. Only Sly Paw, my cat, knows my secrets." He winked and rubbed his hands. "In case I catch one of you children, I'd better show you how to get away before I feed you to the rats. Ho, ho, ho! Magic Mark shall lock my handcuffs."

Sly Paw held the sack open and the boastful giant jumped in.

In the excitement of helping lock Giant Og's handcuffs and fasten the chains, something awful happened. George's conjuring trick fell into the sack too.

Muffled roars came from the Giant. The drums in the orchestra made a sound like thunder.

Sly Paw seized George's hand. "Be quick!" the Cat whispered. "We must rescue Princess Zelda. Hurry!"

They untied the beautiful princess who kissed them both and slipped away. The stage went dark. Only George and the Cat were left standing in a pool of light holding the key to the handcuffs.

Seconds passed while everybody waited. Suddenly there was a bang and a puff of smoke. As the Giant threw off his chains and leapt from the sack, the audience gasped. He'd gone all red. He'd turned into tomato ketchup!

Nobody was more amazed than Giant Og. The Cat couldn't stop laughing.

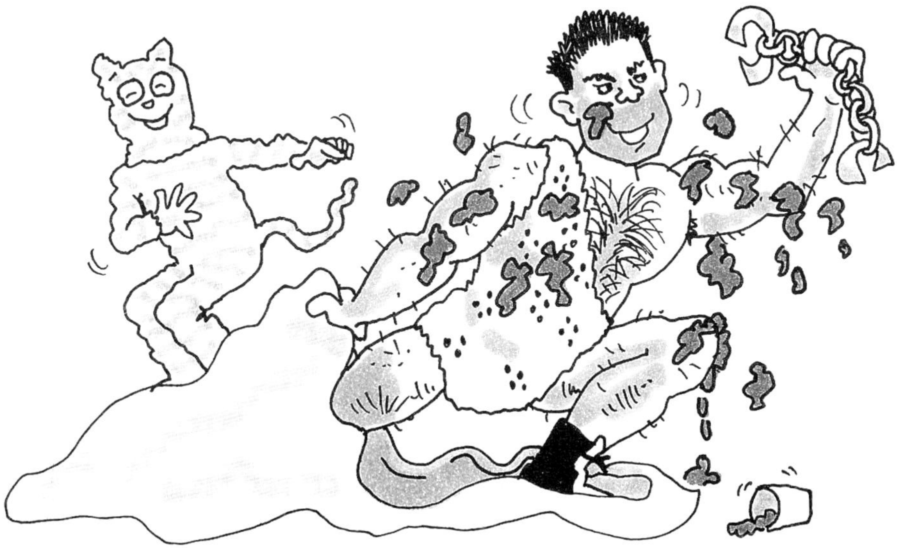

"But how did you do it, Magic Mark?" all his friends were asking afterwards.

"You're a real magician, aren't you," Emily said.

"It was nothing," George replied. "I just said the magic words."

ONLY WUNNY

After the pantomime, George was even more keen on conjuring. He pinned up his signed photos of Giant Og and Sly Paw, the Cat, on his bedroom wall. Sometimes he strode about talking like the Giant in a booming, boastful voice and laughing "Ho, ho, ho!"

George knew the Giant's cat was really a man called Bert in a cat costume, but he often wished he

had a cat himself to keep him company and help him with his tricks.

His mother was too busy. In the mornings she made sandwiches for offices and in the afternoons she cooked food for people's parties. She hadn't got much time for watching tricks.

"But couldn't I have a cat?" George asked his mother for the tenth time.

"Oh dear, not yet," she answered. "How could we look after it properly? I know we live on the ground floor but our flat has no garden and there's such a lot of traffic. If we let a kitten out, it might be run over."

"I could look after a cat," George said sadly. He went to his room and got out his tricks. As he picked up the magic wand, he shut his eyes, trying to imagine the sort of cat it might be. Not a kitten . . . more a big, old fighty cat like Sly Paw with . . . .

"George!" his mother called. "Tea!"

He opened his eyes. There on the window sill, looking in, was a huge ginger cat with one eye.

"Oh!" he said. "Gosh!" He opened the window but the cat was frightened and dived away.

Next day George was eating a Mars Bar and dreaming about being a famous magician when something made him look at the window. The ginger cat was there again.

"Hallo!" George said.

The cat's mouth opened in a sad little O but no sound came out.

"Probably hungry, aren't you?" George suggested and he went to the kitchen for food. "I didn't know I'd wished for a cat with one eye," he thought, surprised.

The ginger cat was hungry. Keeping one wary eye on George, he wolfed down a chopped-up sausage and some liver then he jumped off the window sill. He washed himself over the road outside a boarded-up pub called the Dog's Breakfast.

"Funny, I thought I had a bit of liver left," George's mother said to herself before supper. "How odd."

He didn't tell her about the cat.

Next day half a tin of tuna disappeared and some smoked salmon snacks which George's mother had prepared for a directors' dinner.

The ginger cat was beginning to look better already. He let George stroke him and even stayed on the window sill to wash himself.

"I don't think Sly Eye is a good name really for a

magician's cat," George said. "I could call you One Eye. Probably I'll just call you Wunny."

"I'm glad you've got such a big appetite, George," his mother said, a few days later, "but please don't keep helping yourself. Wait for meal times."

"It's my magic cat," he explained. "He's so hungry."

She laughed. "A magic cat ought to eat magic mice. Now don't put any real food in your conjuring containers or we'll get mice in the flat."

With Wunny about there weren't going to be any mice. As soon as he felt brave enough, he stepped between the window bars into George's bedroom. He sniffed the carpet and all the toys. Then he settled himself on the chair, half-expecting to be thrown out as he'd been thrown out of places all his life.

"Wunny, watch!" George said.

While he did his disappearing egg trick, and conjured silk handkerchiefs from his father's hat, the cat watched with his eye half-closed as if he knew all the secrets.

George daren't tell his mother about Wunny in case she said he had to go. There was no need to tell, anyway.

When everybody was in bed and the flat was dark and still, the cat plopped through the window onto George's bed and lay purring beside him. By the time it was light, he was gone, back to his life in the street.

Things might have gone on like this, but of course all the other stray cats got to know about George as well.

At first it was only a tabby cat with a torn ear. George shared Wunny's food to feed him as well, but soon there was a poor white cat watching hopefully from under a parked car.

Luckily his mother was having a bath as George nipped back to the kitchen. He saw some trays of caviar biscuits and bacon rolls and tossed a handful of those out of the window.

That did it.

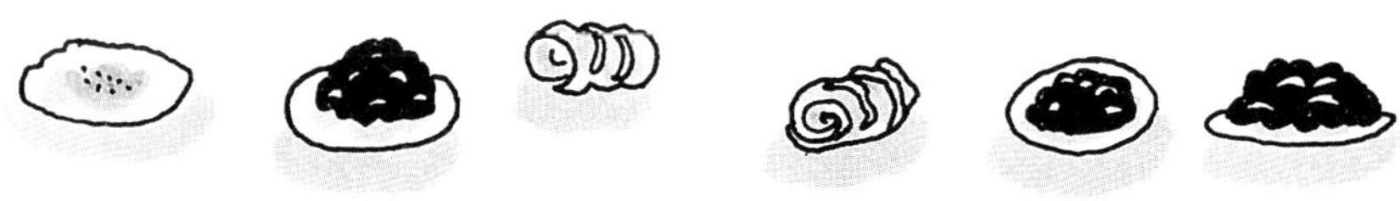

Some more cats came. And then more.

Cats hidden
in bushes,
sitting on walls,
under cars

and behind the boards of the deserted pub. They all waited beneath George's bedroom window for their supper.

"But I only wanted Wunny," he said. He didn't know what to do.

Secretly he scraped leftovers from school dinner plates and took them home in a plastic bag. He spent his pocket money on tins of cat food. When he waved his magic wand, he hoped they'd all disappear like the egg, but they didn't. The mewing mob stayed.

George felt desperate. He waited and watched. The cats got a turkey cooked for the Cricket Club lunch. And when his mother arrived at the Town Hall and unloaded the supper ordered for the Mayor's golden wedding party, half the salmon was missing.

George had never seen her so furious. "I was only feeding my magic cats," he tried to explain. But when he took her to the bedroom window, there wasn't a cat anywhere. Not a torn ear or a hopeful eye. Not a whisker.

"I'm sick to death of that magic set," she said. "Give it to me. I'm locking the kitchen door and don't ever let me hear the word *cat* again or there'll be very serious trouble."

Next day his mother was still in a rage. George kept a fish finger and a half for Wunny but there was nothing for the other cats. When he went to bed he knew they were still waiting.

He couldn't sleep so he talked to Wunny. "Maybe I'll do a paper round. Maybe we'd better run away." He lowered his voice. "Hocus Pocus . . . fish bones choke us," he said, hoping for a miracle but not wanting the street cats to hear the word *fish*. "I wish . . ."

His mother opened the bedroom door. "Go to sleep, George." She screamed as the ginger cat leapt off the bed and escaped through the window.

"What was that?"

"It's only Wunny," George said, sitting up in bed. "I've told you . . . he's my magic cat."

His mother looked out of the window into the lamplit street. Staring up at George's bedroom were sixteen cats.

"Good . . . Heavens," his mother said in a faint voice. "George! But these aren't magic cats. They're real." She went on staring as if it was a bad dream, then she went out of the room.

George lay in bed listening. He heard his mother talking in a low voice to his father then eventually the front door slammed. He heard her steps coming round the side of the house and he held on tight to Wunny.

There was a silence then, so he got out of bed and looked out of the window.

He saw a line of saucers on the pavement outside the Dog's Breakfast. His mother was spooning out helpings of chicken and rice, tuna, sardines. . . .

"Hocus Pocus!" George whispered to his cat.

HAT TRICK

"What are we to do about all these cats outside George's window?" his mother asked at the breakfast table, as she counted out tins of cat food. "How on earth can we afford to go on feeding them? I know one or two have homes but the rest are strays. We can't bring them all in. If we keep Wunny, what about the other unwanted ones?"

"Oh, we must keep Wunny," George's father replied, pouring milk into his saucer and putting it down for the big ginger cat.

"Wunny can stay with us forever," George said.

While Wunny yawned and settled down for a snooze in the window box, George was worrying about all the other cats. He had nothing left in his money box.

Tibby Torn-Ear was sitting on top of his father's car. Shy Whitey was sitting under it.

The black bruiser they'd called Fighty Face was sniffing some rubbish outside the Dog's Breakfast and Teeny Weeny, the little grey cat, was chasing a bluebottle.

Paula was washing Patch on the wall.

"A pity we can't turn my chocolate coins into real cash," George said to Wunny, stuffing six into his mouth. He started to practise his drum for the school band, then he suddenly had an idea.

His mother was busy preparing food for an office party as George picked up his drum, collected his tricks, and slipped out of the flat. Outside the Dog's Breakfast he pushed aside one of the broken window boards and climbed into the empty pub. He chalked up a notice in big letters.

George waited at the pub window with his tricks hidden under a red tablecloth. A cross-faced girl went past, then a man in a hurry. When he saw a smiley woman with a shopping basket, he banged his drum like thunder in Giant Og's caves. She stopped to read his notice.

"Ohh . . . poor cats," she said, opening her purse. "May I see the egg disappear please, Magic Mark?"

"Yes, you can," said George. "HOOH HOOH HAH!"

He did the trick and the woman was astounded.

"Fancy that!" she declared, getting out another ten pence. "Now let me see water changing to milk."

George hit the drum. "Magic Mark will surprise you with another miracle! Only One Eye, my cat, knows my secrets!"

He pointed to Wunny sitting in the window box then he showed her the container of water. He covered it with the red tablecloth and tapped it with his wand.

"Abracadabra!" George shouted and whisked the cloth away. There was Tibby Torn-Ear lapping up the milk.

The woman laughed. "Oh, how sweet! Is she a stray? Can I have her?"

George could see it was a good idea. "I'd better ask my mum," he said. And that was how Tibby moved in round the corner.

The next cat to go was the black bruiser, Fighty Face. An old man took a liking to him and he went to a comfortable basement room with a garden.

George's mother wouldn't let George perform any more in the Dog's Breakfast pub window but, gradually, as word spread, the cats began to find homes. Whitey was adopted by the people next door.

One morning, the little grey cat followed George to school. By the time he noticed Teeny Weeny skipping along, it was too late to go back. He hid her inside his anorak.

"Hang your jacket up, George," said the head teacher, Mrs Butler. "The bell's gone for assembly."

"I've got to keep it on," he answered. "I don't feel very well."

"Wait in the Sickroom then," Mrs Butler told him. "I'll come and take your temperature."

George didn't know what to do. He didn't want Teeny to be turned out or shut up somewhere or lost, so he climbed into the Sickroom bed in all his clothes and hid the cat under the covers.

"My dear George, what *are* you doing?" Mrs Butler demanded, when she came in. "Have you got a pain?"

"Yes," he replied in a weak voice. "And I've got measles too and chicken pox."

Mrs Butler seemed worried. "Poor George, you'd better get undressed. What a pity you won't be able to play the drum today at our school band practice."

He nearly jumped out of bed. "I'll play the drum in here," he answered, trying not to shout. "If you bring my lunch as well, I might be able to eat a bit."

She put her hand on his forehead. "No lunch, dear, give your tummy a rest. Never mind the band. We'll put Emily on drums and you can play the triangle at the end of term concert." Mrs Butler went out of the room, leaving George in a state of shock.

The cat enjoyed her day in bed but George was bored stiff and starving hungry by the time his mother arrived to collect him.

"He's been so good," Mrs Butler beamed as she led the way into the Sickroom. "I'm always afraid something will jump out at me when George is about." She bent over the bed to pull back the covers. "What's that magic word you say, George?"

He clutched the blankets too. "Abracadabra!"

They both tugged. Mrs Butler won. A clawing, hissing, spitting fur ball shot into the air.

Mrs Butler and his mother screamed together. *"George!"* And that's how Park School Primary got a school cat.

Teeny Weeny was everyone's favourite and she settled happily at school, but George was sulking. He was in a bad mood because he didn't want to play the triangle at the concert.

"But *girls* aren't drummers," he scoffed at the final rehearsal.

Emily put her tongue out. "Shut up, stewface!" Then she shut her eyes, and started showing off, banging away like anything. "I'm the best!"

He punched her.

"Go outside, please, George," Mrs Butler called from the piano. "You're spoiling this band for everybody."

"I'm not playing in that band," George told Wunny. He hid the triangle in his secrets box in all the rubbish inside the Dog's Breakfast. "That girl Emily thinks she's so clever. She'd better watch out."

He swished his magic wand about wishing he could put a spell on her. His cat wasn't being very magical either. Wunny rolled over on his back. As George rubbed his tummy, he smiled to himself. He had an idea. Old Emily was going to get a shock when she started drumming.

Next day the children had to prepare all the chairs for the parents to listen to their performance. George seemed busier than anyone. He even stayed late while the others were putting on their coats.

When he woke in the morning, George stayed in bed and pulled the duvet up to his nose. "I feel sick," he said. "I'm not going."

His mother smiled. "Nonsense, we can't miss Parents Day. Up you get. You'll feel better then."

His parents made him go.

"I want to hear that band," his father said as he started the car. Then George did begin to feel sick.

He forgot the triangle and they had to go back. His father fetched the secrets box from the Dog's Breakfast because George was in his concert clothes. He put it in the boot and dusted himself down.

"That old box is so full, I couldn't fit the top on properly. By Jove, it's heavy and riddled with mouse holes. My hat's in there . . . ruined, of course. In any case, I've told you, George, you are not to go into that empty pub."

At the school, Mrs Butler was waiting.

"Quick, George, leave your things here and come with me!" She set his secrets box down beside some other boxes containing prizes. "Poor Emily has 'flu. Will you be our drummer?"

Drummer? Would he!

Dazed, he just nodded, "Sure." In the excitement he forgot the shocks he'd planned for Emily.

When the parents were seated, the band filed onto the platform. Mrs Butler sat down at the piano.

George sat down on a whoopee cushion with a loud rude noise. *Phwff . . . r . . . r . . . t!*

If you go down in the woods today
You're sure of a big surprise. . . .

As Mrs Butler hit the first keys of the Teddy Bears' Picnic, three stink bombs went off in the piano. A clash of cymbals and tambourines drowned the noise.

George was itching.
He couldn't keep still.
He twitched and jumped
as if he had fleas.

His arms flew out and he hit the drum like a madman.

The audience laughed like anything. They clapped and clapped for an encore. Then another.

The concert was a great success.

Afterwards came the prize-giving. George hadn't won a prize but Mrs Butler made a little speech about him.

"There is one child who deserves a special prize for playing the drum splendidly at the last minute. We call him Magic Mark at school because he does tricks but I hope on this occasion he will have put his magic wand away. Come up, please, George!"

The applause was terrific. As Mrs Butler reached for a prize, she knocked the lid off George's secret box. From a flurry of streamers, a hat rose slowly. Underneath was a huge ginger cat. Wunny's mouth opened in a pleased little O but not a sound came out.

"Ohhhh . . . !" murmured everyone.

"George!" moaned his mother.

"It's got my hat on," said his father.

"That's my magic cat," said Magic Mark.